This storybook is for sharing.

Read
Sign
Pass it on!
Lovely

ISBN 978-0-692-24514-9
Library of Congress Copyright 1-1537016541, 2014

PINKYLUXSCHOOLFORGIRLS.COM

What is a Woman?

No one seems to know!
Read on!
Emergency Style!

How it all Began!

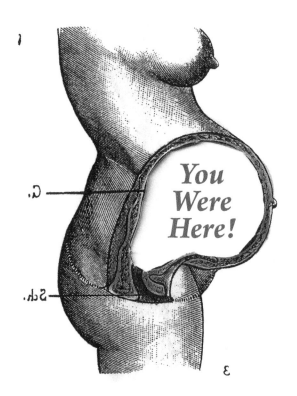

Creation is Not a myth, Not a Story!

There is One True Undeniable Fact -

'You and every person that ever lived came out of the body of a woman.'

This is not a myth, it's not a story, it's not a hypothesis or a philosophy or the result of a government funded study or an opinion poll gathered from a news program. It's not a religious belief, doesn't require faith or a common language and you don't need a class or an ancient text to know this fact. This fact doesn't require a scholar or a professional in the field or a doctor or a comparative study. It's not your **opinion**.

It is the factual beginning of each self. It is the **one fact** *we all share with every person that we engage with in love, hate, jealousy, kindess, judgement, anger, apathy, passion, work, play, sex and laughter, etc.*

You came from the body of a woman.

Women produce **people**.
People are the **product of women**.

You may believe that we came from dust and a rib or the evolution theory or maybe the big bang theory is your chestnut. That's just fine. But our **truest creation story**, *one that we can all agree upon, is that every human that ever loved or died or invented or sang or killed, came out of the body of a woman.*

If this is true for you Turn the page!

So what happens–

Between here

And here!

The greatest mystery in the whole universe!!!

The Pussy Mystery!

How did the fleshy portal by which you were conceived become nasty, hidden and dirty?!!!

Let's take a look!
Fact or Fiction?

The reason you exist is because fluid from a male merged with the reproductive system inside of a woman.

Fact ☐   Fiction ☐

Your body was nourished inside of a woman until you were viable for life outside of her.

Fact ☐   Fiction ☐

The body of a woman is designed to make human beings, care for and feed them and not designed to kill them.

Fact ☐   Fiction ☐

If you checked Fact to any of these questions I bet it makes you curious as to what these amazing creatures feel about the world. What their philosophy of life is.
What! You never asked them!

I hope these profound creatures aren't dancing around like cupcakes or hiding under a bed sheet?

Is it the poo thing?

. . . that makes us think the lower depths from which we emerged is 'dirty and nasty'!

Well let's clear that up today!

We all poo like we all breathe. 'In' to nourish 'out' to eliminate. We eat and drink and the body does this miraculous thing where it chooses self from non-self.

It's doing it right now – **for you**.

The self: it makes into more you! The non-self: it sends out of the body, with breath, with sweat, with urine and with poo.

This poo factory is as much a part of your **brilliant design** as your favourite parts. Poo would love nothing more than to just fall on the ground and continue its journey enlivening the soil to grow things for us to eat that would then create more poo. **You are an entity that creates fertilizer and that is something!**

A good dump is a **sign of health** and enlivens the whole being.

Often as babies, when someone changed our diaper we looked up to see the hideously disapproving face of our mother/father/caregiver calling us 'stinky.'

The reason poo has evolved to smell so terrible probably has something to do with preventing us from eating it – which doesn't stop a gorilla if you have ever been to the zoo.

A friend once told me she was staying at a place in India where, when she felt the urge, she would tear out to the outhouse that was several yards behind the house to try and beat the wild pigs that would come right under her as she let one fly. They'd gobble the poo up like it was a treat from the dairy queen.

So if you are confusing your feelings about 'stinky nasty poo' with the portal where you came from, thinking it is stinky and nasty by association, there is no need – it's just a design issue. And you might even think your own self to be stinky and nasty by association – well you are not.

Now go drop a deuce and give yourself some love!

Will you take the *Porn Test?

pornography - intending to cause sexual excitement

Where does your porn response kick in?

Here?

Here?

Perhaps Here?

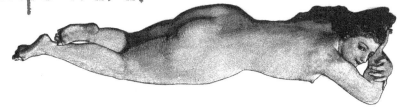

If you picked Mimsy the Fabulous Singing Cat you are not alone!
It probably means that you are always
excited!

Let's take a look!

Sex, digestion and sleep all run off the same nervous system – the parasympathetic. It's as normal to feel sexual as it is to be hungry or sleepy! All these activities are designed to seek a rhythmic balance. Rhythmic?!

What's going on! We are sexed up, dieting, sleep disturbed maniacs!

It seems there is some aspect of our culture that is plugging into our energy and running our show!

Perhaps it's because we aren't given an opportunity to develop ourselves to appreciate our humble, fleshy beginnings. Common cultural humor is the repulsion of the very thought of our parents 'doing it.' Why are we repulsed at the thought of our parents doing something that: created you, improves their health and deepens their relationship to one another?

Repulsed by your very start! Give yourself a chance!

The sexual urge is indeed very powerful. It's a frequency of great hunger that courses through us. It can learn to identify with almost anything for satisfaction, people have become wired to have sex with cars or ashtrays or children!

But there is something more powerful than the urge for sex. It's the **power of an idea**. *It is not even that hard to implant an idea into a mind to the point of convincing someone to kill themselves . . . or others! Shaming, punishing, ostracizing, torturing, murdering . . . for an idea.*

*So **what are your ideas?** Whose ideas are you living? Your own? Your cultures? Your ancestors? What do you think about where you came from – the female body? What do you think about your wonderful body that was made inside your mother? What do you think of someone else's wonderful body?*

Sex is the urge to create. Men are taking pills to make them erect when the body is not able, women are using sexuality to have power and feel lost when it fades. Millions of children and women are being used as sexual slaves while you read this. Children that are all the product of women!

Let's create something else!

And let's use our **sexual energy!**
Sure, why not **it's delightful!**

Look, there you are!

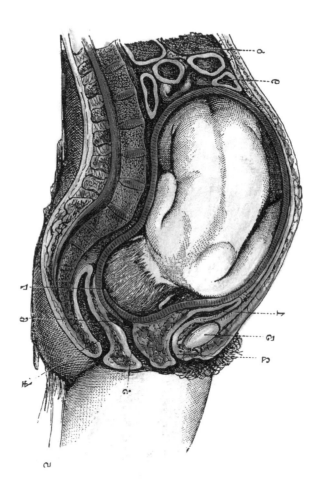

What's that you're nestled in?

It's time to go beyond Vagina!

'Vagina' is the anatomical name of the roadway to the most sophisticated reproduction system in (as far as we know) the entire universe.

Would you say of your car "Wow, my car's tailpipe is great on gas" or "I love my car, its tailpipe is really powerful and has great torque." Of course you wouldn't, how ridiculous!

Here at the PinkyLux School we take up the task of renaming 'the area.' Does it need to be so parsing and mechanistic? **The name of a roadway?!** I wonder who thought that up? Dare a culture embrace a **new name** for their true homeland? Could that begin to unite us, reflect a value to human life that seems missing? Could **changing a word** invite our rabid over thinking into the intelligence of the body? Could woman gain **the power and dignity that their body actually holds?** Could that then bring a uniting compassion to the people that they produce?

Probably not!

But that doesn't stop anyone at this school from **going for it!**

Instead of vagina – the roadway, we refer to the entire reproductive system and call it

'The Undercarriage.'

Why? Because **you** were carried under **the heart of a woman** in this dazzlingly brilliant design. Too poetic?

It's a fact.

Are Women Even Inside Women Anymore?

When you go for a stroll through a park it's common to come upon a statue.

A statue of a man is likely to be dressed in period clothes, have a name and date attached, along with some idea of the deeds he has contributed to society.

A statue of a woman is likely to be an idealized generic beauty that comes not with a name but with a quality like **Justice, Mercy or Liberty.**

This is something you can check out for yourself!

Now, go to an art museum and look at the pictures of women that have been revered by society for centuries. You will find an abundance of marvelous depictions of women predominantly from **the perspective of the brilliant male artist.**

And the histories of the world have little to say about women and children. I guess they were busy doing other things. **Too busy to write about themselves it's certain! Or even learn to write!**

Reading much of the great literature requires a transposing of 'he' for 'she' if a lady is to take the journey of the protagonist. **It's exhausting!**

In our modern culture women are still predominately **drawn from male ideas of women** - don't make me use statistics! Go watch a movie!

We have been taking in 'ideas' of what a woman is for so many centuries while being raised in and living in political/cultural/religious institutions built from a male perspective how is it even possible that real women are still inside women!

I know you are in there!
Thinking Bonnets On!
Emergency Style!

If woman had invented the world

do you think there would be . . .

Roads paved in pink; mandatory afternoon tea and chat time; Piggy Back rides instead of cars; rescue dogs getting the vote; men running around in high heels in hopes of getting a sexy glance; cities designed like **enchanted fairy lands**; older women tossing away their partners for younger ones; buildings **bedazzled by law**; men wearing sheets and hiding in homes while women ride around naked with the wind in their hair; menstrual tents on **every corner**; holidays dedicated to crying.

Then you don't know women at all!

Just as sperm emerges from a man's body, **people** emerge from a woman's body. If a man's body inspires him to build guns, submarines, skyscrapers and pursue imperialistic exploration then it is highly probable that a woman's body would **inspire her to create;**

Political centers that share a wall with a birthing centre; grandmothers having veto power; people living underground and growing food on their roofs; walls and bridges grown from a bacterial batter; hugs would be the only therapy; no computers needed as **woman's intuition** would find a way to connect the entire world; if you had a quarrel with a neighbor you would have to go live with them and eat their food and learn their language, **not kill them;** telling the truth would be so fun there would be no need for lawyers; it would be natural for all bodies, no matter what style, **to have dignity;** electricity would be developed from fireflies and yes . . . there would be lots of dancing to the sound of the wind and things would be bedazzled.

The human body is what **women make.** Everyone's health comes with it; keeping you at 98.6 degrees – no problem; healing cuts and bruises – sure in a jiff! It houses all your thinking! Your body is an innate intelligence that works round the clock **maintaining and building you!** **It's not out to get you!**

Let your body think!

Ladies!

What are the best shoes to wear while inventing?

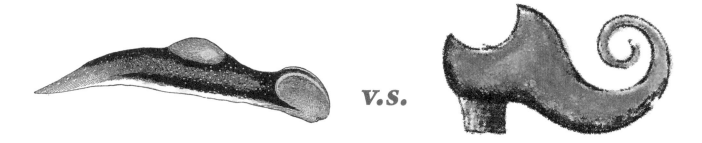

v.s.

Your foot is that thing that dangles off the end of your leg. It's got those wiggly tips that turn out to be perfect for painting pretty colours.

From a Ladies Magazine:

"It's true that surgical procedures such as shortening toes and even completely cutting off pinky toes are increasingly popular choices for ladies who simply have to fit into all those fab shoes."

From Grimms' Cinderella:

"The ugly step sister succeeded in getting her toe into the shoe, but her heel was way too big. Her mother handed her a knife and said: "Cut off part of your heel. Once you're queen, you won't need to go on foot anymore."

Fact: your foot has more in common with a slug than with a fancy shoe.

And you know it!

Your foot is an artist of the highest degree. It's the thing that carries you around – not the Prince! Its joy is to feel where the ground is and give signals to your entire body so that you can balance, counterbalance, walk, move, and dance without even thinking! It registers hundreds of impulses a second and doesn't even bug you about not getting enough praise or recognition for carrying you around willy-nilly here and there.

Barefoot is best! Let 'em spread out and feast on reading the ground!

But when me must shoe, what kind of foot bed is best?

Think for a moment what kind of bed you would want your hands to be in if you made them a bed – a wooden coffin that squeezes your fingers together and deprives them of sensing? Could you yourself nestle into that foot bed to go to sleep? Or would that leave you standing upside down with your head strapped into a box and your back aching?

And your feet will be working while they are in this bed! Doing your bidding all around the town! Ladies must get their heads out of the clouds and their feet back on the earth –

Ordering!
Some moss shoes please!

Do you think your own thoughts?

Let's get a bead on 'you' first.
You seem to be an interactive biological entity.
The basic principle of you seems to be: stuff going in and stuff going out.

Let's check that.

Sperm comes into a woman's body and a baby comes out.
Breath comes into the baby body, goes in and out, goes out one last time and that's it.
Food and water go in, waste and water go out.
Consciousness comes in and you wake, consciousness goes out and you sleep.
Feelings come in, feelings go out.
Impressions come in, thoughts go out.
Information comes in, information goes out.
Experiences come in, memories come out
Education comes in, thinking comes out.
Ideas come in, ideas come out.

So.

Your developing self took in all these experiences with your family,
your culture, your education and mingled it and sorted it and stored it in
your flesh and brain. So here you are, a bag of ideas and theories
and hopes and swirling, competing thoughts!
Tah dah!
Which thoughts are yours? Are you busy thinking other people thoughts?
Of course you are! You are jammed to the roof with them!
Re-thinking is the key!

What should you Rethink? Everything!

Do you think gossip has value? What do you think real beauty is?
How many different kinds of love do you feel? What is love?
Does jealousy have value? Are your prejudices your own?
Are your fears actual? Are the things you think actual facts?

Who is running your show?

I hope it's you!

Let's take a look at Menstrual Blood!

Our ancestors puzzled over blood.
If someone got cut and too much of this substance leaked out the person would die.
When blood stopped coming to a woman for several moons a baby would grow in her.
Blood is the juice that creates life!

Male circumcision began as a rite to give the pubescent male the 'power of blood' in his nether regions. This mimicked the blood that came to a young woman when she began to menstruate, the male emulating this 'magical' and life creating body change that held the power of life.

This view of menstrual blood led to the hope that sacrificing an animal, its blood dedicated to some spirit/god/power, would grant wishes (no judgement).

The bible reads like an endless hack and whack of some lovely farm animals and often people as well. Eg: to get rid of leprosy: sacrifice a ram and two sheep, have their entrails read by the priest and their blood wiped on your right side. Rivers of blood flowed in the temples and on altars worldwide.

People, get a grip, it's just a menstrual cycle!

The next evolutionary Aha! was when someone realized how semen was involved with creating life. I wish I could say this was an improvement but alas, no. Now that men could claim ownership of a child, they wanted to make sure that the child was theirs and began **controlling female sexual freedom**. Nothing hampers a woman's sex drive more than seeing her besties' head get chopped off for having a child while their husband had been years away at war!

Give menstruation a break!

Menstruation is the sign of a healthy body! 'PMS' is a sign you need to improve your health – unless you think you were designed to go crabbing around, getting all weepy and irrational. This myth gets used to deny women responsible jobs and dismiss viable and needed discussions. Why would anyone be taken seriously if they are victims of their 'irrational bodies' purportedly caused by menstruation or menopause!

That's not nature's plan for you, that's your own wacky idea!
The whole world could learn from the rhythm of the cycle of creation you carry – it's exhausted from trying to be run like a machine!

This in no way means you should be waving your tampons in peoples faces! Absolument pas! Menstruation is not a sport!

Ride that rhythm ladies! It's what life requires!
Eat more veggies! Get sound sleep! Hydrate!
Rethink! Listen to your body!

It's trying to love you!

Why we aren't Feminist at the PinkyLux School

. . . even though they are much appreciated!

Here's the thing . . .

It just so happens that our world isn't running on the systems of thought that women have developed.

Quickly . . .
. . . Name 3 women philosophers. Name 3 religions started by a woman.
Name 3 systems of government developed by a woman.

Sigh.

Did you know that most physical movement systems were developed by men and on the male pelvis? That includes Yoga and Ballet. This is wonderful and no one here is upset by that. At the PinkyLux School we just want to add to what is already here, not yell at it as it's in very rough shape!

And add we must!

How about a new system of math! No woman can truly embrace a math that declares a family can have 2.5 children!

Math is simply a language that explains something. I will make one up right now from my Undercarriage. *1 +1 = 1*

Adding 1 thing to 1 other thing makes it part of 1 group. True? Yes it is. It depends on your perception. A woman can be a slut or a potential for new ideas, it's up to you to decide!

The first seven years of a child's life determines a great deal about who the adult will be.

A woman's philosophy would include children and most likely not include raising them to think that undercarriages were nasty!

Where is this system of thought?

It's coming.

From you!

Everybody is Everything!

Here at the PinkyLux School *we* **don't parse men and women up** *by insisting that they each have male and female qualities. We call bull.*

Check it out.

Here are some 'typical female' qualities;

dependent, emotional, graceful, weak, nurturing, soft, passive, receptive

Here are some 'typical male' qualities;

independent, non-emotional, aggressive, competitive, strong, unyielding

Surely you recognize yourself as capable of having all these qualities **no matter what gender you are** because they are human qualities. The more we associate these qualities with one gender or another, 'she's so male because she is aggressive,' 'he's so feminine because he is nurturing' the more we restrict and build in prejudices and limitations to **the full palette of each person.**

Calling a man a 'Big Girl' should be a compliment!

Why can't a man crying be a sad man and not 'someone showing his feminine side'? Why can't a sexually aggressive woman be a passionate woman and not a 'has a sex drive like a man' kind of woman? It can be so! With this one simple adjustment we can eliminate all sorts of stereotypical judgements towards those that come out of a woman's undercarriage. A woman is a woman with all the human qualities and a man is a man with all the human qualities and a transgender person is a person with all the human qualities . . .

Everyone is human, having human qualities!

Lovely

Let's Take a Look at the Female Ego!

It's very popular to try and not have an ego these days.
The ego gets a very bad rap and many people feel it is the root of many
problems – egotistical, full of yourself, my ego made me do it – there are even
classes on how to get rid of your ego!

Well, Ladies, here at the PinkyLux School we want you to do no such thing! The female ego hasn't even had a proper debutantes ball into society yet and it becomes popular to not have one.

Ego – 'the part of a person that is conscious and thinks; the self'

We must bring into full fashion the true 'Female Identity' and let the world get a load of how innately intelligent and wisely kind women are.

The first to realize this of course will be you!

It's time to bring out your real Ego!!!

Start identifying with the vehicle you are cruising around in – the greatest creative collection of protoplasm the world has ever known. No more whining about your menstrual cycle and how someone doesn't understand you or know how to love you.

You have bigger fish to fry.

I know it has been tough what with the Barbie doll as an ideal and living in a world that has been built in thought, word and deed by the hard work of the male of our species.

Wait a minute!

Every one of those males was grown in the female body! Nice work!

If culture had been curious to listen to the harmony and rhythm of the womb from which they came from to expand our world, what lives would we be living?

Add your true female ego to the mix! Be 'full of yourself'!
The world needs you!

Yup!! Women, Gossip and Criticism!!

It's time to take a look at **excavating** that pernicious veil that culture tosses over us as a survival tool – **criticism and gossip!**

Gossip is a currency of cruelty that we are taught to use as a way to empower ourselves by bringing another person down!

Most often a lovely lady!

Gossip is part of the culture of competition where we make a 'winning' or 'losing' out of every choice that another human being makes as they attempt to live out their bag of tricks that they were handed as a child. Gossiping is a way of shaming and criticizing in absentia and boy does it feel good! Tasty morsels of **'I am right'** delicious bonbons of **'aren't we better than,'** glorious chats between people that are bonded by the common cause of diminishing another while harvesting a feeling of winning!

No wonder women struggle to have a voice! They are being nitpicked about their every move by other women! It would be quite shocking for women to **become known for discourse over new ideas** that aren't about nail polish, body image or someone else's business!

You know what's in your conversation.

Stop trying to make Men and Women Equal!!!

Must we keep seeking equality that is measured by a system that is in direct need of a makeover?
Why are women trying to be equal to men?

Maybe men should be trying to be equal to woman!

But wait!

What does society show us about women – gossipy, menstruating romantics that live for a diamond ring. Bad at math creatures who are taught that being accepted comes from controlling your appearance so you can then control others with it. That shopping is a skill equal to inventing. That love is getting someone to do what you want. No wonder we are trying to be equal to men! Even though the system that defines what a 'man' is puts men in a misogynist mind state! So women are trying to be equal from inside a philosophy that establishes them as objects to be managed.

Can this battle be won?

Romantic comedies continue to show us that if a man stalks you and tricks you he will eventually 'get' you.

One of the greatest movies ever made 'The Godfather' is the story of a love struck young woman who falls for a man with a big fun family who keep her in the dark about how she lives in luxury and gets a smack when she steps out of line.

Let's stop trying to force women to be equal to men. Men aren't all that super happy with the pressure and often perverse values that are hanging around their necks!

Bring forth new ideas, a political system, an economic theory, art and stories and shove them down our throats because we need female designed thought to stand up and inspire us into a new way of being together. Where men, women, children and pregnant woman are considered and respected and supported by reason that is born from . . . reason!

There is a hole in the ozone.

Your voice is missing.

. . . and stop raising children to be Heroes!!!

Let's raise them to be mothers and fathers instead!

'Mother' and 'Father' the verb!
To mother, to father.
Not to save the world but to take care of it!

Not bunches of punches but listening!

Imagine, Industry being run like a family! Not **your family! A functional one!**

Government leaders who were mothers and fathers first would rethink sending children off to go **kill other children!** *Ce n'est pas possible!*

Everyday, mothers and fathers suck it up, get over it, accept and move on, **dig deep,** *go beyond, rise above,* **figure it out,** *push to the limit, push some more, invent a way, make it happen, pull it off, hope for the best, stand up, hold out, hold on, try again,* **never give up, embrace, hold, struggle.** *Why?*
Because love trains them.
Too corny? Not ironic enough? Not 'winning'?

Not to be rude but you are here because nobody managed to kill you. However hideous you might feel your childhood was I bet there were more 'heroic' moments in caring for you than in all the super hero stories ever told.

Mothering and Fathering are an attitude, a point of view, a perception. They are not gender or age specific and can be applied to anything and anyone. They are part of your basic package in the art of being human. They are probably the reason why you like all those cat pictures. They offer; being bigger than your circumstance, including all, accepting people as they are, looking for the best in someone, patience, laughter, grit, gratitude and the most nurturing sets of eggs and balls you will ever encounter.

Isn't that enough?

Do you suffer from Genital Concern?

**The Prime Minister of Canada, Pierre Elliot Trudeau, once stated,
"The government does not belong in the bedrooms of the people."**

If you disagree with this very reasonable statement then perhaps you are suffering from

Genital Concern.

Do you find yourself concerned about other peoples genitals? What they look like?
What they might be doing? Wondering what they might do next?

Someone else's genitals is none of your concern and you know it!

We have the LGBT people to thank for **inspiring us to rethink** our conscious, unconscious
and ancestral ideas about what our business is in regard to sex, freedom and love.

And perhaps most importantly for driving the evolution of consciousness into a place where we
train ourselves to look at the humanity of each person. To look past gender and fashion and
color and class and size and shape and haircut and right into the beating heart of each person.
To meet one another on an even playing field of shared humanity.

Millions of people have been challenged to **rethink** because of this community!
Perhaps you are one of them!

Rethinking is an activity that your brain enjoys because it is **designed for growth!**
Sure exercising and stretching the old noggin can activate your 'frisky resister' but just like
your ham strings it needs exercise, you feel better for it and you'll improve with practice.

We all come out of the body of a woman.

We all carry nature's hope.

Upgrade your Grampa thinking!

The universe is expanding and we hope you are too!

Are you just a tad more interested in upgrading your wardrobe than your thinking?

Sure we inherited eye color and limb length but we also inherited the thinking styles we were surrounded by when growing up. You might not be caught dead in a pattern that your mother wore but how about the pattern of her thoughts? Check and see if you are sporting a brain bonnet from yesteryear!!

'The Grampa Grouper' is when someone fails to individualize, 'All pit bulls are dangerous,' 'Women are bitches before their period,' 'All Canadians are sorry.' This kind of lumping **leads to prejudice** and missing out on the truth of each human's uniqueness.

'Saintly thinking' is when you think you are right for someone else. You are right for you and that is plenty. Someone else is right for themselves, suck it up. Healthy discussions are welcome. Being kind and right is very advanced!

'The 100% er:' You don't have to be 100%! The internal pressure to be 100% can feel like a ton! And it leads to being critical of yourself and others for not being 100%. What is 100% anyway!! Life isn't a pop quiz! 100% is a measurement that grew inside you that no one can see **and keeps you busy managing and judging the whole universe!**

Oddly, many people who claim not to be religious have these hangover habits that were often formed from religious thinking!

Did you read this with your old thinking? Tricky isn't it?

Burkas are Bad for Men!!!

Let's Take a Look . . .

Just the other day I saw a lovely lady walking down the street in some comfortable shorty shorts and a bit of a tee shirt. She was glowing with health and freedom. She had no cares in the world – she wasn't even on her cell phone! Sometimes a man passing her would glance at her and sometimes a man wouldn't. Everyone was just going about their day!

How can this be! Aren't men driven mad by the sight of a lovely lady almost naked enjoying a stroll in the sun? Isn't she at risk of being violated? Isn't she a whore and a slut and ruining the world with her smooth gams? Controlling men's minds and driving them away from healthy thoughts and deeds? No, she is not! Millions of ladies worldwide enjoy the sun on their skin and the freedom to dress as they choose. And men live respectfully among them!

Men can just as easily be conditioned to manage their sexual urges as to be ruled by them. Men everywhere are doing it every second all over the world!

Good job men! Thank you!

Freedom of dress for women allows men to adjust themselves as they grow into their sexuality. Hiding women denies men an opportunity to evolve their sexuality and frames them as weak and unable to develop themselves beyond animal instincts. It disrespects their innate strength to adapt and mature.

Men! We know you are good evolvers!

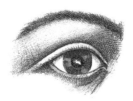 *You prove it everyday.*

Money and the Undercarriage!!!

This world trembles **with the spirit of money – haunting, lusty
money with the power of a religious force.**

I know you feel it!

Money is supposed to be a symbol of work done, of labor but it has run amok and become so many different things – a game, numbers on paper, power, generosity, love, fear, security, greed, sex, confidence, happiness, freedom.

We are feeding the GNP when we shop! We are nourishing the world in some direction with every dollar saved or spent. The GNP is at our breast!

We are all mothers feeding the world!

Who is a mother? Sure you had one but you might be one and not know it! Are you 'one who mothers'? Can you 'bring something up with care and affection'? 'Mothers Against Drunk Driving' did not give up until they had created a law infused with the care and affection that they knew so well.

It's too bad that Mothers and mothering are not more popular in the business and political world. A corporation is certainly not a person as it most certainly did not come out of a woman's undercarriage!

It's a good thing that 'mothering' isn't interested in being popular and has a great internal engine that can stay the course and get things done. We are all 'bringing up' the world at this very moment!

Let others have a snack and nap while we organize and vote!

Do you think mothering is too soft, too namby pamby to turn this ship around? Then you don't know mothering. Mothers are fierce! It's not the time of the great mother mythical spirit, nor the goddess, it's the time for actual mothers, real mothering, from you – your care and affection and grit and grace.
Our time to bring up the world is now and you know it!

Let's gather.
The world will tremble at our vote!

So, what is a woman?

A woman is someone who gave birth to you.

*We are all truly 'womankind' – the kind that come from
the body of women.*

*A woman is wearing the design that nature developed for new life to be made in.
Nature loves her for just being here. She is designed for patience, caring and the
grit for what it takes to raise a life on earth. A woman carries the greatest ability
for innate nurturing intelligence that we know of. Aren't you curious about what
her ideas for living are?*

*Do you ever wonder what a woman feels when what she is designed to
produce – children – are sent to kill other women's children? When countless
of 'womankind' are starving when there is enough to eat and drink for all and
the problem is distribution? When the image of her kind is daily raped and
murdered, in reality and on countless screens and stories?*

It gets a Lady down!

*Can women even hear their own deep wisdom anymore?
The answer is yes, yes they can.
If they* **listen for it.**

If you **listen for it.**

If you looked at this picture and saw a lovely lady relaxing in a bath you have been schooled!

This woman chose to give birth to some wonderful new ideas!

Nice work!

Is it you?

What we all have in common.

All of us began inside a woman and sport a body that breathes air, needs water and nourishment. Nourishment from food, from others and from knowledge.

Our differences come from our perceptions.

They can be changed.

Wendel Meldrum is an award winning actor who has worked with similar themes in her movie *Cruel But Necessary*, her ebook *Notes from the Undercarriage* and on her blog 'PinkyLuxSchoolforGirls.com.